AMAZING PARENTING

All parents can be great parents, its a journey and we will get there

Amazing Parenting For Dads

By Grace Chukwu

© Copyright 2018 Grace Chukwu

All rights reserved

This book shall not, by any way of trade or otherwise, be lent, re-sold, hired out, or otherwise circulate without the prior consent of the copyright holder in any form or binding or cover other than that in which it is published and without a similar condition including this condition being imposed on the subsequent purchaser. The use of its contents in any other media is also subject to the same conditions.

Contents

Acknowledgments 1

To All The Dads 3

1, Discipline 5

2, Super Dad 11

3, Treat Mum Well 15

4, Love 19

5, Fun 23

6, Don't Leave 27

7, Your Story 33

8, Prayer 37

9, Provide 41

10, Protect 47

11, Role Model 53

12, The Friends You Keep 57

13, What You Say 61

14, What You Do 66

15, Hero 70

16, Hands On 75

17, Parents Evening 79

18, Wash The Car 83

19, Seen But Not Heard 87

20, On Your Shoulders 92

21, Friendships 96

22, Work Life Balance 100

23, Daddy's Girl 104

24, Football 111

25, Champion 117

26, The Future 123

27, Dad In Prison 127

28, The Head 131

29, Don't Hold A Grudge............................ 135

30, Hard Work... 139

In conclusion.. 143

Acknowledgments

I would like to acknowledge and thank three fathers in my life.

My husband, Daniel Friday Chukwu who is the father of my two children and continues to do a great job.

My pastor, Matthew Ashimolowo (KICC) who is a father figure to thousands around the world.

And of course my father (daddy) Thomas Aidoo who is and will forever be my hero. He taught me priceless lessons and helped me be the woman and mother that I am today.

I salute you.

To All The Dads

All the books I have written are for both parents; mum and dad, however I have wanted to write this book for a while. If you have read my other books you will know I was brought up by my dad, who was and still is my hero. Dads, you have a special role to play in the lives of your children, equal with their mother. Sometimes dads are relegated to the back ground because mums can be so formidable.

Your place, as dad has been set, immoveable, stationed and steadfast, since the beginning of time. But you have to make a conscious effort to maintain this.

Dads, you must always step up to the plate and be counted as a worthy contributor to your family. This book will highlight areas that are important for a healthy relationship between dad and his children. Seize the challenge of being a dad.

These thirty pieces of advice are to add to your already arsenal of tools that will enhance your endeavours to being a great dad.

1, Discipline

1, Discipline

In most households, it's the dad that the children listen to first time round. Mum may have to shout several times before she is heard, or should I say listened to. Dad doesn't have to always raise his voice; sometimes a look will calm the storm. The children will know it's time to settle down.

Dads, you have a way you can be with your children that is just baffling. You can walk into your home or pull into the drive and the children automatically start behaving, or sitting up straight, doing home work or at least look like they are doing home work. However this power can be over used to the point the children only see dad as a disciplinarian.

The trouble with that is the children don't see you as anything else. Dad you have to have a balance where your children know you for being stern when you need to be but playful and approachable at any other time.

This doesn't have to be difficult to deliver, just be conscious that you have not had much fun time with your children and incorporate it at the next opportunity.

For example, your children are playing nicely together, join in and make them laugh, sit with them or just add yourself to the conversation, better still ask them if they want ice cream.

Feel free, to hug, kiss, high five your children for no reason other than you love them and want to show it. "I love you" should be normal for your children to hear you say on a regular basis.

There is a misconception that if you say I love you too many times, it will make you soft. This is not true, how many times in your life, childhood and adulthood that you heard the words I love you and thought the person saying it was too soft?

Discipline is a must have in any home and it should not be shielded away from because your child cries or sulks when they get told off for behaving badly or pushing boundaries. When discipline is not used, it is a matter of time before the children are ruling the household, becoming a nuisance in the community or at school.

Discipline can spill over and get violent, this should be avoided. Children can interpret being smacked as a way of dealing with their own anger when frustrated with friends or siblings.

Children are moldable and correct discipline such as removing toys, gadgets and privileges will work, it can take some time but in the long run you and your children will see the benefits.

2, Super Dad

2, Super Dad

Just like superman he was not wearing his cape all the time. He was sometimes Clark Kent. He only became superman when he needed to be.

There will be times in your fatherhood when you will do great things for your children; it may not be as dramatic compared to the events as superman but none the less it will be great. Your children will look back over their lives and remember all the time when you were there for them and did what only dad could do.

You may see yourself as an ordinary dad, like Clark Kent and that's ok because ordinary is good for every day.

However, I use the term super dad also for the dads who are doing it alone, single dads. My dad was a single dad and that's all I knew from a very young age. It was when I became an adult and especially when I had my own children when I realised how super my dad truly was.

How he juggled work, home, cooking and us all at the same time, he was awesome, it could not have been easy for him, but he persevered through it all, resisting giving us up to the care system.

We hear of single mums all the time and we doff our hats to most of them. It is rare that we hear or see of single dads in the community raising good children.

If this is you or someone you know, well done, your reward may not be seen immediately but it is coming you can be sure of that. To be a single dad can be very difficult because where do you go for support; it's not as if there are lots of them at the school gate dropping of their children for you to have a chat with.

There are groups and organisations that do support single dads. You don't have to be isolated or suffer in silence. Your children need you to be strong so they can be who they need to be and reach their best potential.

Whatever reason you find yourself as a single dad, may it be the death of your wife, relationship breakdown or mental health issues, know the best person for your children to be with is you, their super dad.

3, Treat Mum Well

3, Treat Mum Well

How you treat your children's mum speaks volumes. What you say to her and what you do to her will be embedded in your children's minds forever.

Your son will learn from a young age how to treat his wife, rightly or wrongly and your daughter will know how she is supposed to be treated by a man/husband. You are so instrumental on how your children perceive adult relationships.

Don't think your children are too young to notice how you treat their mum; they see and hear more than you think. They may not be able to articulate what is going on but they know if it's right or wrong, even if wrong becomes the norm.

Your children's mum is where they receive a lot of their nurture from and if mum is not in a good place because dad is constantly treating her badly or just not good enough, it can translate to the children not getting what they need from her on a regular basis. For example if dad is always calling mum names or shouting at her or even hitting her, how will she be able to care for the children adequately?

Your children trust you to do the right thing and when you don't, it is very confusing and damaging for them. It is only a matter of time before what they have seen or heard begins to take its toll on them.

You may have witnessed your dad treat your mum badly and you can see how it has affected you in your adult life. You have received firsthand what is like to see or hear a mum treated badly. This is all the more reason to treat your children's mum well.

Treating mum well is beneficial for you, her and the children. It makes for a harmonious home life which will reflect at school and into your children's future.

4, Love

4, Love

Your love, as dad for your children is unique. The only part you played to their being born was their conception. They did not grow in your tummy inches away from your beating heart but when they were born you loved them as if you did carry them for nine months.

A father's love needs to be seen, heard and felt by his children. Don't relent in this area; don't give up any room to bitterness or drawn out anger, especially when your children get older.

Your children see your love by what you do for them, not necessarily what you buy them, your time with them is priceless. You may not be able to give them your time every day but the quality of time, they will never forget.

Your children hear that you love them by you saying so and giving words of admonition and praise, yes your admonition and correction is a show of love. If you let your children get away with whatever they want, what you are basically saying is "I don't care what you do"; in the long run your children will grow up out of control. Not being able to show much love themselves.

Your children feel your love by you hugging and kissing them, showing them affection. As your children get older the hugs and kisses may lessen but your terms of endearment don't have to. A heartfelt text message from you, a high five or pat on the back will still go a long way in the department of love.

All of these outward displays of love are needed from you to your children, regularly. Love is like food; your children cannot do without it. You would not starve them of food, so why starve them of love?

5, Fun

5, Fun

This is a big area in today's society, finding time for fun. As dad, you must create a culture and cultivate an atmosphere of fun. It must become the norm in your house and your children will look forward to this time with you.

This does not mean you don't correct your children, let them know you are not happy with their behaviour or take away their gadgets and treats. It means your children see two sides of you, the fun side and the stern side.

There is nothing wrong with dads having these two characteristics as long as it doesn't come out as Dr Jekyll and Mr Hyde, where it's one extreme to the other. Make fun and discipline part of your lives.

Ask yourself when the last time you and your children laughed together was. When last did you play hide and seek with your preschool child or take your teen to see a film in the cinema, or are you too old to hide behind the curtains or do you think every film in the cinema is full of sex, drugs and bad language.

The answer is no, you are not too old and not all the films in the cinema are bad. There are so many ways for you to have good family fun with your children, no matter how old they are or how old you are.

As dad, the time you spend with your children will be remembered for a life time and when you run into tough times in life, it's your memories that keep you and your children going.

Ask your children what they want to do for fun and go with the flow, you will know if it is too daring or too pricey and it is ok to say so and then look for an alternative.

6, Don't Leave

6, Don't Leave

It is a sad day when a dad leaves his children because of one reason or another. A divorce or separation from your spouse/ partner is devastating for children, they just don't understand why, most of the time. Their heads and hearts can be messed up for a very long time trying to work out what they did wrong, even when they are told it was not their fault.

A lot of children carry this hurt into adulthood and if therapy is not sort for, these children can become confused adults, lost and searching for answers, looking in all the wrong places for relief, such as alcohol, drugs, sex and violence. The feeling of rejection is immense for some of these children and handling rejection in later life can be devastating. For example a simple job interview rejection or a dinner date rejection can spiral out of control into suicide or other harmful tendencies.

Now, I'm not here saying don't get divorced, that is your decision and you have the reasons. What I am saying is don't leave your children. You have left their house but don't leave their lives.

Your life with their mum has ended but you will never stop being a dad, your relationship with them doesn't end. You must keep in contact by all means. If your children are young and their mum does not trust you any more, then seek legal advice. If your children are teenagers, you still may need legal advice but if there are no contact issues between you and their mum, then arrange to meet your children regularly or text them. Make sure you go to all the school activities, such as parents evening, sports day and the Christmas plays.

Continue to be a part of your children's life, make all the necessary effort to show them that you have not left their lives and you still want to be a big part of it.

Try to be amicable with their mum, for your children's sake, not hers. Cutting your nose off to spite your face will only hurt your children. They need your presence even more. Share the school holidays as equally as possible. If their mum finds a new man, then deal with that as a mature adult, you will probably find someone new as well in time.

Never bad mouth your children's mum in front of them. You may need to vent and get things off your chest. No matter what she has done. If your children are very young they will find out the truth later on and if they are already teens by the time of the separation, then they probably know what happened between you.

Children are very loyal to their parents and hearing one spoken of in a derogatory manner will only cause them pain, even if they don't show it to your face.

Mum and dad relationships are not for children to suffer from but to benefit from even in the worst situations.

7, Your Story

7, Your Story

You, dad are a conglomerate of experiences, wisdom, knowledge and intelligence, all of which make up your life story and your children need to hear it.

Your story can be told in part at different stages of your children's life, exciting parts of your life, your childhood, how you met their mum, how you managed difficult situations, trouble you got into that you could have avoided, good and bad influences, the list goes on.

As you tell your children about your life, you are passing on meaningful times that they will relate to in different seasons in their own lives. There is a bond that takes place when you tell someone something special, great, sad or touching, and what better bond to have that with than with your children.

When you do this with your teen, it may trigger a conversation that you may not have had if you had not told them a small portion of your past. Your life story may not be able to be told in one sitting and that's ok.

When your children are young, using your childhood experience as bed time stories can be fun, just make sure it does end happy.

Your life story is worth hearing and you may be pleasantly surprised at your children's response.

8, Prayer

8 Prayer

Praying may or may not be your thing, you may or may not be a religious dad, however it is one of those things in life we are grateful to have someone pray for us and it can make others feel blessed when received.

When you say a prayer for your child it is not in vain whether they are in the same room as you or across the globe. A praying parent is heard by the one who can bring that prayer to pass.

If you are not a praying dad, don't look at prayer as a religious thing but look at it as added support. There are some issues in life that your children will be in that you will not be able to solve and all you can do at that time is pray.

Prayers don't have to be long, you don't have to close your eyes or clasp your hands, just mean it with all of your heart and as a dad that will come easier to you than you think, why? because that's where your children sit, in your heart.

It takes a strong dad to know he needs help sometimes for his children and it takes even a stronger dad to humble himself and realise prayer at such a time is needed.

9, Provide

9, Provide

This is a must for all dads whether you live with yourchildren or not, whether you've gone on to have more children elsewhere; you are obligated as a dad to provide for all of them.

You may have had children by "accident", when you were too young and did not know better, never the less, you are now a dad and as long as you know that they're yours you must provide for them.I have known of cases where mums have not wanted any provision from their children's father due to break down of relationship, however, that is not a mother's call, that doesn't mean you must not provide, even if you put something aside for your child when they are older than you can give it to them.

Just think if you put £1 a day away for your child from the day they were born until they were eighteen years old how much money you would have saved for them.

Provide, is not just monetary, that is to provide love, understanding, care, wisdom and time are all needed from a dad.

When your children come to you for provision don't point them in the direction of their mum, you be the one to supply their need.

You can get to a point where children don't even think of asking their dad for anything they bypass him and go straight to their mum believing that their dad cannot provide what they need because mum is always providing for them and when they do ask dad for anything he says "go ask your mother".

For your children to see you as a provider you have to be prepared to provide for them. When your children ask you for something that is within your means and it is a necessity for them to have it, you should be the one to provide it, for example you may not be the one who necessarily goes out to buy the goods but you must make sure mum or your children have the means to buy what is needed.

Provision also extends to your children's mum, what she needs and requires you should also provide her with the money, time affection, listening ear and being an all-round provider. Let your children grow up with an understanding with the memory and the knowledge that their dad always was there to provide what they needed- school uniform, bedding, sports equipment, etc.

Dads, you must be ready to deliver what your household needs.

Even if you are a dad who iscurrently out of work, your provision comes in the form of contribution for example in the shape of cooking, cleaning, helping children with their homework, bath times, school run and so forth.

Dads, don't minimise the level of your provision it is all needed, wanted, required and beneficial to your children and family.

10, Protect

10, Protect

Let's talk about the physical side of protect. As a dad you protect your children from harm, you make sure all the windows and doors are locked in the evening once everyone goes to bed to protect them from intruders.

You hold your children's hand when you cross the road to protect them from traffic.

You keep them safe when you take them swimming by putting arm bands on them and keeping close supervision.

You would defend your children if someone wanted to hurt them.

All forms of physical protection are needed and must be put in place, however there is also emotional protection that dads need to give their children;for example this can come in the form of, protecting your child's innocence.

I hear parents say they allow their children to be exposed to certain things such as sex, violence and profanity, because they're going to see and hear that in the world anyway. There is a time and a place for your children to be exposed to certain things and while they're still young under your roof that is not the time for them to be exposed to things that will take away the early innocence. As a dad you need to be protecting your children's innocence because once it's gone, it's gone forever. And another reason why you need to protect your child's innocence is because nobody else will. The media, society, the government, nobody really cares whether your child loses their innocence early or late in life, so as a dad you have to ensure your child's innocence is protected.

Also you have to protect your child emotions. When your child is in need of emotional warmth, emotional stability and emotional care, you have to be prepared to minister that level of emotion to your child. This may come in the form of reassurance, acceptance, praise; all these things cultivate positive emotional development for your child.

If you think back to your own childhood where you may or may not have received emotional warmth, stability, encouragement and how it has affected you. How youemotionally protect your children will pan out later in life, when they too need to be emotionally aware. When emotional protection is withdrawn or withheld it affectschildren negatively, they can be cold emotionally or have no empathy for others and find it easy to be mean. But as you nurture your children you will see the importance of emotional protection.

Another area of emotional protection is in the area of teenagers, when they want to start dating and are interested in the opposite sex. You are protecting their emotions by explaining the pitfalls of dating too early and how their emotions are not ready for adult relationships.

Let's not be fooled by thinking teenagers are not going to do things that are not emotionally led by peers, media and fashion. However as dad, you'll have to explain, teach and encourage your children the correct way to conduct their lives so their emotions are not damaged.

Physical and emotional protection starts from a young age. The younger your children are when you begin to introduce it will make it easier to implement and cultivate the environment of this kind of protection. It then will become normal and natural for your children to hear you when you begin to talk about emotional protection as they get older and peer pressure tries to set in.

11, Role Model

11, Role Model

This sounds obvious but as a dad you need to be a positive role model for your children. This gives your children no excuse to misbehave in life because they had a good role model.

Yes, sometimes children do go off the rails when they get older but don't let it be because you were a poor role model and they copied your mistakes.

How many dads do you know that are not the role model they need to be for their sons and daughters? How it affects their children negatively. Being a role model is not just being a dad, it's every aspect of your life your children can look up to, be happy about and want to emulate when they are older.

You being a role model for your children is seen in how you talk, dress, conduct yourself in and out of the home, how you handle tough situations, how you treat and respect their mother. Do you behave one way with your friends and a completely different way at home?

As a role model you can't afford to be hypocritical, your children see you all of the time, When you wear a suit and tie and when you are in your PJs, when you think they're not looking and listening, they are.

Just like you want to be proud of your children, your children want to be proud of you. They want to be able to say "that's my dad!" or "my dad will help me" or "my dad can do that".

It's ok for your children to have TV role models in the shape of sports men and women, or well behaved celebrities but you dad have to be right up there when it comes to personal hands on role models.

Children need their dads to be positive male role models more than they need any other TV personality.

12, The Friends You Keep

12, The Friends You Keep

The friends you keep say a lot about you. Depending on the age of your children, ask them what they think about the friends you invite to the house or the friends that they know you associate with. What your children see in those friends, why you have them as your friends and what they bring to you as a friend. You will be surprised how insightful your children are about your friends.

I once knew a dad who had a friend and this dad's son knew this friend was not good for his dad. This friend, whenever he came round to their home; he would smoke weed and drink alcohol and even though this dad did those things, his son knew this friend always encouraged his to do these things even more.

Do your children like your friends? Are they happy when your friends come to visit? Are they even happier when they leave?

Who you associate with will either lift you up or take you down and if your children see you aspire to great friends and people, that's the kind of friends they are going to want to hang around with, but if they see you have friends who are demoralizing, depleting, take from you, leave you sad, make you angry, join you to get drunk, well that's the kind of friends they're going to have.

If you are keeping friends who are not good for you, what message are you sending your children? When they are pressured with their friends and begin to hang around with the wrong peer groups' that try to lead them astray, friends who want them to do the wrong things, if you as a dad also have such friends how will you begin to influence and direct your children to stay away from such friends.

Your friends don't have to look or be like you, but they should have and support the same values as you. You should be able to leave your children with your friends and know they will come to no harm, physically or emotionally. Your children's mother should be comfortable with your friends.

Your friends should be good for you as well as you good for them.

13, What You Say

13, What You Say

You don't need me to tell you; your words are powerful, just listen to any motivational speaker and they will tell you how great your words are, and how words shape your life.

What you say to your children will have a long lasting profound effect on them; that doesn't mean everything you say has to be profound however the words of a dad are priceless. What you say to your children will count positively or negatively. You are the first man your children will hear. They hear your male voice through their mother's womb.

Never use what you say to put down your children, words like,"you're stupid","you're foolish","you're worthless","you will amount to nothing","I regret having you". You may feel these things; towards your children but never put voice to something that is a negative feeling. The feeling will pass but the words will last forever.

There is a saying that"sticks and stones may break my bones but names will never hurt me". That saying is a lie. What you say to your children can destroy them mentally, emotionally and even physically. It can cripple potential, dreams and abilities.

What you say can wreck your relationship with your child or enhance your relationship.

When your child becomes an adult, that's when you may realise what you have said has positively impacted them or negatively impacted them. Things you said when they were five years old that you may have forgotten about, may still lay heavy in their hearts and has formed their personalities and character.

You don't have to be a loud dad or a big bad dad for your words to be significant. Just say what is needed.

By not shouting or swearing or putting your children down by using derogatory names doesn't mean you are a pushover dad, on the contrary, it means you know the importance of your words.

By being a dad who is mindful of his words, makes you far more powerful than a dad who uses brute force in his words and deeds. Your children are more likely to listen to you when you are stern and serious, and when it's time to give those words of wisdom and truth, they will take it on board.

14, What You Do

14, What You Do

In the previous chapter we talked about what you say, well what you do is just as important as what you say, why? Because your children are watching you even when you think they are not.

What you do carries weight with your children for good or for bad. I once knew a mum who was a smoker and her fifteen year old daughter started to smoke and the mum was so angry with the daughter for smoking. I said to the mum "why are you angry at your daughter for smoking"? The mum replied, "she's too young to smoke she shouldn't be smoking". I said to the mum "but you smoke", and the mum said "I'm an adult I'm allowed to smoke".

Just because something is legal doesn't make it right. Getting drunk in the comfort of your own home isn't illegal, having sex outside marriage doesn't give you a criminal record, but is it right?

If you don't want your child to do something fundamentally wrong, then you should not be doing it, whether you are an adult and 'allowed' to do it. That's the mindset you need to have when you are doing things as a parent.

As dads, when your children watch you do something, even though they know it's wrong, they will either gravitate towards doing that thing or possibly dislike you for doing it.

A child may see his dad hit his mum and know this is wrong but when he becomes an adult and is angry with a woman he is more likely to hit her than to think I need to walk away because it is wrong to hit a woman.

There are children who grow up to become adults, who do terrible things that their parents never did, my answer to this is, you, as dad do the right thing, when your children are living under your roof. When your children become adults they have to choose to do what is wrong and it won't be because they saw you do it.

Being conscious of what you do will put you in good stead for yourself as well as your children, for life.

Your behaviour as dad is crucial to your children's wellbeing and all round growth.

15, Hero

15, Hero

I once knew a dad who was, in my eyes, far from being a hero but when I saw his young children look at him, he was their hero. He didn't live with them, he didn't give their mum regular money even though he worked full time, he didn't take them out on a regular basis but when his children saw him they hugged him, loved on him and wanted him to stay. In their eyes they saw a hero, he was their hero.

When your children are young you are their hero, they look up to you, they listen to you, they want to be with you, they want to be like you and that's great. However if you have not been a 'sound' dad, your hero status will fade very quickly as your children get older.

When your children hit those teenage years and for some dad's that can be a battle in itself, but for you to maintain your hero status you must be consistent. Your children must know you to be consistent. Let your yes always be yes, and let your no always be no. It might get really rocky but if you maintain your relationship with your children being there for them, understanding them, having fun with them, being strict with them when needed and showing them love. You then will come out on the other side and you will still be their hero.

I would describe it like this. There are invisible strands from children to their parents and when children are very young the strands are very thick, they are there in abundance and the strands are made up of beliefs, truth and knowledge that children hold about the their parent. But those strands get severed and frayed when you break a promise, when you call your child a name that you never should have, when you are mean to their mother and so on.

The strands get broken when you knowingly do something wrong and your child sees or hears you do it. The strands get broken when your habits are out of line with your words. As your children get older; maintaining the hero status can get harder but what keeps those strands from breaking, what keeps those strands strong is doing what's right which means, when you keep your promises, when you say what you mean and mean what you say and when you love them openly, those invisible strands stay strong, stay intact, stay full and stay voluminous.

Your hero status may fluctuate over the years but when your children have children, you will know whether you did a good job or not.

16, Hands On

16, Hands On

One of the best things you can do for the mother of your children is be at the birth of your children. This prepares you for being a hands on dad. Just the length of time it can take to give birth, teaches you patience.

You may not have been there at your son or daughter's birth. I remember when our son was born my husband wasn't there. He was asked to leave the operating theatre because there were major complications at his birth and even I was unconscious when he was born. You can read that story in one of my other books. My husband not being physically there at my son's birth didn't stop him from being a hands on dad.

Hands on dads are so needed in this society. What do I mean by a hands on dad? It's a dad who does not shy away from any of his responsibilities and is happy to take on new ones. He can do his daughter's hair, cook dinner, tidy up and bath the babies, read a bedtime story, do the school run and anything else that is needed.

In more and more homes now, mum and dad work full time, which means the running of a successful home is in both of their hands.

When a dad recognises his role, his role is defined by what is needed to be done in his house to make it run smoothly, his whole family benefits from it.

If you ask any mother what makes her children's dad great, she will most likely say, he helps raise the children up with her equally.

You, as dad are worth your weight in diamonds when you do the simple, basic and everyday things well.

17, Parents Evening

17, Parents Evening

Parents evening happens at least once a year throughout your child's school life. It is imperative as a dad you are there.

It's not only good for you to hear how well or not your children are doing but it also lets your children know you are just as interested in their education as their mum is.

You want to know, you want to hear and you want to see what's happening at school. Where your child needs more support, where they are doing exceptionally well, and how you as dad can help them to excel.

It also shows school that there is an active dad in this family. Too many dads are absent at parents evening leaving it to the mum to gather all the information and relay back to dad in between the busyness of the day.

If you need to take time off work, if you need to reschedule a shift then that's what you need to do to attend parents evenings.

Your child's school life is not only about academics but it's about their wellbeing, why? Because they spend more waking hours at school then they do at home for the majority of their childhood.

Your input is needed and when your child talks to you about school and certain teachers you have a handle on what's going on. Your child sees you take their school life serious, which in turn will help them to be more conscientious about their work.

Even if you no longer live with your children and are not on speaking terms with their mum, you can always schedule a time that suits you, where you will not bump into each other. Parents evening goes on for hours, as dad you must make the effort to attend.

18, Wash The Car

18, Wash The Car

As your children get older it's important that you find things to do with them and washing the car is one of them. My husband would wash the car with my son; they would get buckets of water (this was before I bought him a pressure washer for Christmas) and car shampoo and be away for a couple of hours washing my car and his car.

You might not have a car to wash but there are so many other things you can do together. Sometimes your teenagers will come up with ideas for things to do. Go along with it where possible. Sometimes they they'll be happy to stay in their room and play on their phone or on the Xbox, so you'll have to come up with creative ideas to get them out or stay in the house and do stuff, either way you must have things to do with your children on a regular basis.

You might say, everything your teenagers want to do cost money, well that's where you need to get creative, not everything that they want to do costs money, it's just that you may not have explored or thought of things you can do that doesn't cost much money or any money. Here are a few ideas.

Play the Xbox together, window shopping, internet surfing, play games at the park, watch a DVD, play a board game, walk the dog (it doesn't have to be your dog), clear out the garage, go and watch a Sunday league football match, (there is normally one taking place in some local parks), go for a walk, talk about favourite topics, have a thumb war, paint the garden fence. The list goes on and on.

The more things you can do with your children the better your relationship will be with them. As your children get older and may want to do less with you, allow them to take the lead and go with the flow.

A teen with a parent positively involved in their life will be more unlikely to get mixed up in gangs and other unsocial activities. When a dad is visibly present in his child's life, having fun and doing things together, the child wants to do more with his or her dad.

.

19, Seen But Not Heard

19, Seen But Not Heard

This has to be one of the saddest kinds of dads, a dad who is seen but not heard. I was watching a documentary on gang warfare and the host of the programme was interviewing a gang member and he asked him about his family and he said his dad was at home but really didn't do much.

Some dads think and feel as long as they pay the mortgage, bring money home to buy food, keep a roof over everybody's head is enough. They can just bury their nose in the newspaper or in the laptop or put their feet up and watch TV and leave everything else to mum. This cannot be the case, if your children are going to grow up and have good memories about you.

A dad who is seen and not heard can sometimes be even worse than a dad who is not there at all physically.

As a dad in the home your children need your input, they need to hear your voice, they need to see and hear you be active in their lives. Dads that are seen and not heard put too much pressure on the mums, even if she is superwoman and can do it all.

Too many mums are burning out due to not being able to cope with their teenage son who don't listen to her because they are going through their 'alpha male' stage or her daughter is staying out late doing things that she shouldn't be.

A seen and not heard dad gives his children the impression that he does not care or love them enough to get involved in their lives. This leaves the children thinking and feeling they don't have to care about the important things, like family life.

You may feel your voice doesn't count because your children's mum is superwoman and does everything and controls everything and is capable of doing everything. That is not the point; the point is you are dad and the facet you bring to the home can only come from you.

Your physical and emotional male presence with your children and family is immense and once withdrawn is detrimental to the wellbeing of your home.

As dad you must endeavour to be heard, seen and listen to.

20, On Your Shoulders

20, On Your Shoulders

When your children become adults they need to be far better off than you ever was, not just materially but mentally, emotionally and yes, financially.

When you see a child sitting on his dad shoulders the child is looking far into the distance, the child is happy, they're always smiling, they look content, they look like they are on top of the world and I'm sure that's how they feel.

But your children can only go further than you; if you equip them with the tools, knowledge and the understanding. Teaching your child to be resilient is one of the greatest things you can do.

Standing on your shoulders means your children see further, wider, high and their expectations are greater, their desires are bigger, their motivation and hunger to be their best is better because they stood on your shoulders.

When your children stand on your shoulders you give them an advantage, you put them in front, ahead, on top.

Your children may not understand in the beginning when you are pushing them to do better, try harder and insisting they behave in a certain way but it will all make sense to them in the end.

Your children standing on your shoulders means you have to pour yourself into them consciously, tirelessly and lovingly.

A dad that does this will never be poor, in any sense of the word. The son of a dad that does this will be strong, kind and responsible.

The daughter of a dad that does this will respect herself and be a pillar to those around her.

A dad that does this will be kept 'warm' in his old age.

A dad that does this will never be far from his children's hearts.

The dad that does this will always have grandchildren and great grandchildren to play with.

A dad that does this will be remembered for generations to come.

21, Friendships

21, Friendships

Know your children's friends. There comes a time in a teenager's life were they are influenced more by outside the home then sometimes inside the home.

As dad, don't shy away from asking your children who their friends are and why they're friends with that person.

Your children's friends are playing a part in your child's life, whether you believe it or not, whether you like it or not and if you don't like the influence your child's friends are having on them let your child know. Don't wait until your child is completely wayward due to bad company before you intervene, your child's life can depend on your stepping in.

Some children have been led astray by gangs and riotous living all because a parent turned a blind eye to what looked like regular friends and teenage behaviour. The moment you suspect your child hanging around with no good friends, for want of a better word, you need to take action.

Action does necessarily mean you come down hard, because this can also back fire, but start with reasoning conversation, hear what they have to say about their friends and then give your input, advice and continue to monitor the situation.

Sometimes dad's feel like they don't want to interfere with their children's lives, they don't want to rock the boat. Like we said a few chapters ago your children need to hear your voice, they need to hear your opinion and your reasons, and so it's important that you enquire about your children's relationships and friendships.

22, Work Life Balance

22, Work Life Balance

From the beginning of creation, man has been working, it is inbuilt for men to work.

When a man doesn't work he cannot function well, whether he is a businessman, bus driver, gardener, or even a househusband, men have to work.

Men receive a lot of validation and value from their work, there is a sense of achievement and a job well done.

Families are blessed by dads who work. When you as a dad work, you are teaching your son the responsibility of providing for his family. When you as a dad work, you are teaching your daughter, the man she marries has to be working, it is a minimum requirement for a man to be working.

However working is not the be all and end all of life. If all you do is work and spend no or very little time with your family, how will you ever bond with your children?and if there's no bond with your children what relationship will you have?and if there is no relationship with your children what future will you have?

When your children say "Daddy you don't take me to the park anymore","Daddy you don't read me a bedtime story","Daddy I don't see you anymore","Daddy you are always at work" it is time for you to take stock, take a break and spend quality time with your children.

I heard a famous football manager say in an interview when he came to the end of his career and had won trophies, championships and leagues. The interviewer said to him "Do you have any regrets?". The retired football manager said "I wished I spent more time with my children".

Don't allow that to be part of your story. Don't come to the end of your life regretting. It's not your job, your achievements, your accolades, that will be gathered around your bed when you're in your 100s, ready to meet your maker, it will be your children and your grandchildren, those that you've poured your life into, those that you spend quality time with that would be there for you when you close your eyes for the last time.

"Aim for work life harmony"- Jeff Bezos (Amazon).

23, Daddy's Girl

23, Daddy's Girl

When your daughter is born the majority of the people who come to visit will be women. Women such as her mum's friends, aunties, grandma and sisters.

You are the first male voice she hears and you are the first man she knows, she learns about the male species from you.

What you do as a man will resonate with her for life. You are her benchmark for all men, so it is highly important you show her right, teach her right and guide her right.

It can be so easy for young girls to be led astray by boys and men because the male role model they had in their life was either weak, nonexistent or mean, so the first boy that comes along and shows her any interest, she will gravitate towards him.

You have to reinforce her self-esteem through a correct image of who she truly is. Don't let the world define your daughter, don't let the world define her beauty or her intelligence. She is not second-class to a man she is born for a purpose and you as dad must help her get to that purpose and fulfil that purpose. **You tell her how great she is, you boost her confidence.**

This means as dad you have to be the one to take her out, pay for hairdressers to get her hair done, tell her she's beautiful, and call her princess. So when a boy shows up, a standard has already been set, she cannot be bamboozled by a boy telling her she has nice eyes or she's pretty- no, she's heard it all before, from her dad.

Talk to your daughter about boys and the importance of keeping her virginity even though it's not popular. Talk to your daughter about teenage pregnancies and the pitfalls of having a boyfriend too early.

A relationship between a daughter and her dad should be based on trust, openness and honesty. This will only happen, when your bond with your daughter is strong and this starts from the moment you hold her in your arms for the first time.

While your daughter is still living under your roof be that positive male role model in her life, let her know she is not cheap, she's not worthless, nor is she weak because she's feminine.

Champion what she is good at and what she is good at will turn into something that she's brilliant at, which she can turn into a business, a career or a ministry. Academics might not be her thing, it doesn't matter, if you champion her dreams, visions and aspirations she will soar to greater heights.

When my daughter was very young and I went back to work I showed my husband how to do hair in the mornings ready for nursery and he was able to do it. He did the school run, took her shopping, bought her clothes and he still does all of that, but not her hair, I don't think she would let him.

Even if your daughter does not live with you because of marital breakdown or relationship separation, you can still be a major male role model in her life and so you should be, nothing should stop that from continuing.

Being there for your daughter is crucial, being there doesn't necessarily mean your daughter is in a desperate situation and you turn up, being there simply means you're there to cheer her on at her football match, you take her to piano lessons, you go to her Christmas play, you go to sports day, she's having a hard time at school and you are a shoulder to cry on, she doesn't get the job she wanted, you are there to spur her on to fill in more job applications.

No matter how smart your daughter is or becomes, always remind her that her smartness should never out shine her kindness. There is no amount of wrinkle cream that can cover up a mean woman.

And when it's time for boys to come on the scene,and the wedding isle is set before you, be sure to have vetted the youngman very well. Letting him know your daughter's hand is not just for man.

24, Football

24, Football

The reason why I have called this chapter football is because most sons and dads watch football, talk about football and play football, even if it is just kick about in the park.

But whatever you and your son have in common use it to your advantage. Maybe football, golf, gaming, fishing, boxing or Star Wars, whatever it may be, use it as a springboard into your son's world.

Just as in the Daddy's Girl chapter, champion your son's gifting and his talents. Let him know that you've got his back, watching him perform, watch him do what he does best, being a positive voice, but he knows you are his number one fan.

When a son knows his dad has his back it gives him such confidence, zeal and it will be easier for him to stay focused, especially in those teenage years when the pull for his attention is coming from all directions.

When you have a strong relationship with your son it makes it easier for him to take instructions from you even when he doesn't want to.

Your son needs you more than you think and more than he will probably ever tell you. In today's society where young men are falling short because of the lack of positive male role models,sons need to look to their dads for guidance, inspiration, understanding, love and support.

Boys need to learn resilience, staying power and don't give up attitude, when times are hard and it looks like things are not working out. They hold on because they see their dad with the same attitude.

When sons don't get that required help from their dads they can sometimes buckle under the pressures of life and succumb to the temptations of none lasting solution such as drugs, crime, alcohol and sex.

When you let your son know you care about him and not just his grades, he sees you in a different light and pushes himself extra hard to make you proud, at the same time he knows his best is good enough for you.

As your son grows into a man you will see how your relationship becomes watertight and unbreakable even in the tough times. He will find it easy to talk to you about private and delicate matters of the heart.

The relationship he has with you is different to what he has with his mum, so make it count for something special.

25, Champion

25, Champion

Teach your children not to be afraid of failing but to be afraid of not trying. The feeling of not trying should outweigh the feeling of failing. Failing is just a way of knowing how not to do something. And if you learned something when you failed, well, you didn't really fail, that is a lesson all children need to know.

As dad you may do all the disciplining, you may be stricter than your children's mum, you may be the one who puts his foot down, but when it comes to championing your children's gifts talents and abilities you have to be on point.

Every one of your children is a star at something and it's your job to find out what they are a start at and draw it out of them.

Go all out, spend the time, spend the money, and make the effort. Let your children know you are proud of what they're doing.

When a dad champions his children he gives them wings to soar, he gives them the ability to believe in themselves, he gives them the advantage above their peers. You may not have had the relevant support growing up.

Don't let what you are not good at stop you from seeing how far your children can go at what they are good at, instead help them master their gifts and talents, help them take it to the world stage, help them be number one at that thing that they are excellent at whatever that may be, whether it's academics, sport, media, music, entertainment or the arts. The thing that matters more than the job your child does, is the lives they will touch while doing it. Their impact in the world is what will count.

Encourage your children to listen, watch and read up on people who are achieving greatness in the areas of their endeavours. Help your children see nothing is impossible for them if they dedicate themselves to their passion in life.

It's so great when a young person wins or achieves something outstanding and the international news cameras are there to capture it, as a young person thanks their parents for supporting them.

Champion your children to work on their strength and not necessarily their weaknesses help them do what they love and their weaknesses will become irrelevant.

You may have never achieved what your children achieve but what greater sight, then to see your children go further than you ever did.

When children reach their pinnacle in life, more often than not it is a direct reflection of their parents input over the years. What a joy.

26, The future

26, The Future

This is one of the reasons why you are a dad, to prepare your children for the future. Encourage your children to see their future better than their past. How you prepare your children for their future depends on the kind of dad you are and the kind of dad you've been. You want your children to look back over their past and realise what a great dad they had.

You want your children to remember more good times with you than bad; times of laughter, fun and of course correction and discipline. The values you have taught your children, you want them to go on and teach their children the same values. For example, kindness, respect for others, love, and so on.

As dad you want your children to have indelible memories of you, memories that only a dad could give. Now, it's important that you write a Will and if you haven't, do it as soon as you can however a wise man once said, "It's not what you leave to your children, it's what you leave in them." Yes the material belongs you leave your children, such as your wealth or riches, all that is great but it is the non tangibles that will last forever.

27, Dad In Prison

27, Dad In Prison

It is one thing to regret something but it is completely another when you're living your regret day by day incarcerated.

Being in prison is about making choices and as a dad that's one of the key areas you want to teach your children to make the right choices. You are living first-hand as an inmate because of the choices you made.

A dad in prison isn't just hard on the dad but on the children as well. This chapter is not about pointing the finger or laying blame. This chapter is about staying focused, getting out and living the life that will make your children proud. You can't turn the clock back but you can make a change to live a better life.

While you're in prison make it count, don't let the devastation of being in prison consume you, learn all you can, learnatrade, do an exam on line, and work towards getting out early if that is a possibility.

If you can write to your children and you have access to them write them regularly. Let them know you're thinking of them and looking forward to seeing them again.

It can be very worrying and scary for children knowing that their parent is in prison. Some children have seen films where inmates have been beaten up and treated cruelly and this can play on children's mind and cause them to behave negatively, be fearful, aggressive, with drawn and feel helpless.

Whether you're guilty or innocent of the crime, the fact remains you are away from your children and this is having an impact on them. Your release will either lay heavy on their hearts or be an exciting time they're looking forward to.

Use visiting time as an optimistic event. Interact with your children positively.

28, The Head

28, The Head

You are the head of your home as dad even if society does not paint that picture.

For you to realise the reality of you being head you may have to do everything in this book and then some.

Being the head sounds great and powerful but it comes with huge responsibility and the reason why some dads fail at being the head is because they don't take on the full responsibility.

Being the head of anything, whether it's an organisation, a football team, a family, a business or a school, it takes a tremendous amount of staying power, understanding compassion, patience and love.

The issue arises when some dad's want the title and recognition of being the head but don't take on the work that is involved, thus creating problems in the family.

The bigger problem to this is when dads relinquish their head position and leave the family home and leave their children. Society begins to fracture, children begin to go astray, and mums are heavily burdened and overwhelmed.

Now, this is a huge mess in society with absent fathers. This can be traced back and be the main cause to a high percentage of children who don't reach their potential.

When a dad is not in his position as head in all areas, physically emotionally, mentally and financially, his children begin to wither and attainable goals for his children become impossible.

The complication arises because children find their identity in their dad and when dad does not take his headship seriously enough his children and family suffer.

This happens for many reasons, one of the reasons is dad's dad wasn't there to pass on his identity and importance of values, thus the cycle perpetuates through generations. But dad you have to break the cycle, you have to bring the change, you have to make the difference. Step up take your rightful place and be the head of your family.

29, Don't Hold A Grudge

29, Don't Hold A Grudge

Sometimes there are instances between a parent and child's relationship where things are said and later regretted. Things are done that shouldn't have been done. Parents need not to hold a grudge against their children.

That might sound obvious but when tensions are high and arguments have been had, nobody wants to make the first move to say sorry or say I forgive you or it was my fault.

Parents must make inroads to their children even though it's difficult even though it may be hard even though it may not be you to blame. There comes a point when blame and fault are no longer the issue but reconciliation, forgiveness and love needs to come back into play.

I know of parents who had fallen out with their older son due to not seeing eyeto eye on a particular issue, it caused an upset and him leaving the family home.

This doesn't mean you don't get upset or angry with your children and need time to think things through. Dad you should always seek reconciliation over the thing your son or daughter did to upset you. If they don't want that reconciliation, leave it a while and then come back to it, at least you tried.

Holding a grudge against your child whether they are young or adult, it just consumes precious time that you can't get back. You don't want a situation where years have gone by and you are now missing out on the joys of grandchildren. It's not worth it, is it?

30, Hard Work

30, Hard Work

It is very hard to teach your children hard work if you yourself are reliant on government handouts.

The importance of hard work is right up there with teaching your children rules boundaries and routine.

Many children, especially those in their teenage years shy away from hard work simply because it's hard work. Dad, you have to instil and encourage your children to put in the hard work to whatever it is that they do, whatever it is that they want to pursue in life.

If your child wants to be an athlete, you know the hard work that is required for them to be the best. If your child wants to be a best-selling author, even though you've not written any books, you know how much work it's going to take for your child to get onto the New York Times best sellers list.

Teaching your child staying power and hard work is priceless; it's what will differentiate them from their peers.

Yes of course there needs to be rest and play especially when you're dealing with children but when your rest and play outweighs your hard work then success is not going to be in your future and that's what you need to teach your children as dad.

There must be something your children work hard at, whether it's in the classroom or the playing field. What's going to help fuel your children working hard is watching you as their dad work hard.

In conclusion

Dads, take a hold of this great opportunity and be the difference only you can be in your children's lives. Make your presence count for good. Be heard, seen and enjoyed.

I watched the funeral of Billy Graham the great evangelist. His son, Ned gave a speech in less than one minute about his dad and what he said was very wonderful and thought-provoking at the same time.

He said to the listening mourners "I want you to know my father was fat. He was Faithful, Available and he was Teachable".

My question to you is "Are you a FAT dad?"

Go all in, hold nothing back and be the hero that you are!

All parents can be great parents, it's a journey and we will get there!

AMAZING PARENTING

All parents can be great parents, its a journey and we will get there

www.amazingparenting.co.uk

More Books in the Amazing Parenting Collection

Printed in Great Britain
by Amazon